Headwork Stories

Book One

Chris Culshaw

Oxford University Press

Oxford University Press, Walton Street, Oxford OX2 6DP

Oxford New York Toronto
Delhi Bombay Calcutta Madras Karachi
Petaling Jaya Singapore Hong Kong Tokyo
Nairobi Dar es salaam Cape Town
Melbourne Auckland

and associated companies in
Berlin Ibadan

Oxford is a trade mark of Oxford University Press

© Oxford University Press 1987

First published 1987
Reprinted 1988, 1990

ISBN 0 19 833380 3

Set by Pentacor Ltd, High Wycombe, Bucks

Printed in Great Britain
by The Alden Press, Oxford

The illustrations are by Allan Curless,
Kenny McKendry, Richard Maris,
Janet Pontin, and Kate Simpson

Cover illustration: Kate Simpson

Contents

1	The Will	4
2	The Ghost at the Crossroads	8
3	The Tickets	12
4	The Foolish Brothers	15
5	The Fur Coat	18
6	Lost!	22
7	Five More Minutes	27
8	The Ghost that Could Not Rest	31
9	The Lost Ruby	35
10	The Storm	40
11	A Bed for the Night	46
12	The Dark Divide	50
13	A Hundred Thousand Keys	55
14	The Man Leopard	60
	Note to the teacher	64

The Will

Mr Conran was a very rich man, and very mean too. When he died he had £20 million in the bank. He made all his money by selling very sticky sweets. His nickname was "The Dentist's Friend".

Mrs Conran had died ten years before. Mr Conran had only two relatives, his sons Joseph and Oliver. Joseph and Oliver were twins, identical twins. They were so alike that nobody could tell them apart. Not even their father.

Joseph and Oliver had left home when they were 20 years old, and they had never been back. They had never seen their father, or heard from him since they left home.

When the twin brothers heard about their father's death, they went to his house right away. Their father's lawyer, Ms Madoc, was there to meet them.

She said, "Come into the library. I must read your father's will."

They all went into the library and sat down. Ms Madoc took a piece of paper from the desk.

She said, "Your father made a very short will. It is in three parts. Part One says: I leave all my money to my son Oliver."

The lawyer turned to the twin brothers and said, "So which one of you is Oliver?"

Both the sons said, "I am. I'm Oliver!"

Ms Madoc looked very angry. She said, "But you can't both be Oliver. One of you must be a liar."

Both the twins said, "He's the liar. I'm the real Oliver!"

The twins argued and argued. Each called the other a liar and a cheat. Then they started to fight. Ms Madoc had to pull them apart.

She said, "I think I'd better read you the second part of your father's will. It says: If there is any argument about which son is the real Oliver, then I leave all my money to Joseph!"

Once again the lawyer turned to the twins and said, "Which one of you is Joseph?"

"I am!" cried the two sons with one voice.

The lawyer got very cross. She banged the desk with her fist and said, "But a minute ago you both said you were Oliver!"

"I was telling a fib," said one of the twins.

"No—I'm the real Oliver," shouted the other.

They argued and argued for nearly an hour. Both twins tried to prove he was the real Joseph. But Ms Madoc would not believe either of them. She called them both liars.

At last Ms Madoc said, "I think I must read you the third and final part of your father's will. It says: If both my sons, Oliver and Joseph turn out to be liars, then I leave all my money to Ms Madoc, my faithful lawyer."

So the twins left the house without a penny. The clever will had shown them both to be liars and cheats. But it wasn't their father who had tricked them. It was Ms Madoc. You see, all the time she had been reading the will she had been reading from a blank piece of paper. Mr Conran never made a will.

What to do

Are these sentences true, false or is there not enough evidence?

1 Mr Conran owned twenty sweet factories.
2 He was always giving money to charity.
3 He never got married.
4 Joseph and Oliver were 20 years old when their father died.
5 Ms Madoc had worked for Mr Conran for twenty years.
6 Ms Madoc had never seen Joseph and Oliver before.
7 The first part of the will said that Joseph should get all the money.
8 Ms Madoc was very pleased when the twins started to fight.
9 The twins thought that their father had tricked them.
10 Ms Madoc had destroyed Mr Conran's real will.

What to do next

If Mr Conran had made a will and *you* had been his lawyer how would you have found out which twin was which?

The Ghost at the Crossroads

a story from Ireland

Nobody from the village would go near the crossroads after midnight. Everyone said the place was haunted. Lots of people said they had seen a white figure there—a horrible one-eyed woman with a big black cat.

One night, Tom and Mick were in the village pub having a drink. They were talking about the ghost at the crossroads.

"I don't believe in ghosts," said Tom.

"I bet you won't go to the crossroads, by yourself, after midnight," said Mick.

Tom laughed and said, "I'll go—if you will."

So the two men agreed to meet at midnight at the crossroads.

Tom wanted to play a trick on Mick. He went to the crossroads just before midnight. He took a bag of flour and put it all over his face and hair and clothes. Then he sat down on a big stone by the crossroads and waited.

It was a very dark night. As the village clock struck twelve, Tom could hear Mick coming down the road. But he could not see him.

Then he heard Mick calling, "Tom, Tom are you there?"

Tom didn't speak. He sat on the stone, very still and very white.

When Mick came close enough to see Tom, he took one look and ran off down the road screaming, "Help! Help! I've seen a ghost!"

Tom laughed so much he fell off the stone.

Early the next day, Tom went down to Mick's house. Mick was in the kitchen. He had locked all the doors and windows. He

had a shot-gun on the table. He opened the door and let Tom in. Then he locked the door again. He was tired and frightened. He had not been to bed.

"Well," said Tom trying not to laugh, "did you see the ghost last night?"

"Oh yes," whispered Mick, "I saw her as plain as day."

Then Tom said, "You fool! That was me you saw sitting on the stone by the crossroads!"

"Oh yes," said Mick, "I saw you on the stone, and I also saw that evil one-eyed witch with her cat, standing right behind you."

When he heard this, Tom went quite white, as if someone had dusted his face with flour.

		Tom	Mick
1	Who said he didn't believe in ghosts?	1		
2	Who suggested they should have a bet?	2		
3	Who went to the crossroads at ten o'clock?	3		
4	Who went to the crossroads just before midnight?	4		
5	Who disguised himself as a ghost?	5		
6	Who got a terrible shock at midnight?	6		
7	Who spoke to the ghost?	7		
8	Who didn't sleep a wink that night?	8		
9	Who tried to shoot the ghost?	9		
10	Who locked himself in the house?	10		

What to do next

Draw a picture to show what happened at the crossroads at midnight. Label it clearly.

The Tickets

Mr and Mrs Waters had a rabbit farm. They lived in a big house in the country, three miles from the village of Bellstone.

One morning, Mrs Waters was reading the paper when she saw an advert for a travelling circus.

"Look," she said to her husband. "There is a circus coming to Bellstone tomorrow."

"I haven't seen a circus for years," said Mr Waters. "Why don't we go to see it tomorrow?"

"All right," said his wife.

The next day Mr and Mrs Waters got a nice surprise. There was a letter in the post and inside were two free tickets for the circus.

"I wonder who could have sent them?" said Mr Waters.

"I've no idea," said his wife.

So that night Mr and Mrs Waters drove into Bellstone to see the circus. Their seats were right on the front row—two of the best seats in the tent. They had a perfect view of the ring. They arrived just as the show was about to start. There was a tall man with a beard sitting next to Mr Waters. As soon as the show started, this man got up and left.

"That's odd," said Mr Waters.

"Perhaps he wasn't feeling well," said Mrs Waters.

The show was great. Mr and Mrs Waters went home feeling very happy. But when they got home they had an awful shock. Someone had broken into their house. The place was in a

terrible mess. Every room in the house had been turned inside out. The robbers had taken money and silver and jewels.

Mrs Waters 'phoned for the police. Ten minutes later Inspector Hutchinson arrived. He looked round the house. Then he said to Mrs Waters, "Did you go to the circus this evening by any chance?"

"Why yes," said Mrs Waters.

"And did you sit next to a tall man with a beard, who left early?" asked the Inspector.

"Why . . . yes," said Mr Waters, "but how on earth did you know that?"

* * *

Inspector Hutchinson caught the thief who had robbed Mr and Mrs Waters. The thief made a statement telling the police how he had planned the robbery. Here is the beginning of his statement:

```
First I bought a newspaper which told me
when the circus was coming to town.
Next I looked around for a big house in
a lonely spot not too far from town.
I soon found out how many people lived
at the house. Then I ....
```

What to do

Copy the beginning of the statement and complete it in your own words.

What to do next

How did the inspector know that Mr and Mrs Waters had sat next to "a tall man with a beard who left early"?

The Foolish Brothers

Barry and Keith were brothers, but they were always arguing. They argued about money, they argued about the weather, they argued about anything.

When Barry and Keith had a row, it was always Barry who came out on top. One day Keith said to himself, "I've had enough of this. I'm not going to let Barry push me around any longer. I'll show him."

Barry and Keith owned a jeweller's shop in the high street. The next day a customer left the shop door open and Barry told Keith to shut it.

"Shut it yourself!" said Keith.

"I'm busy," said Barry.

"Busy doing nothing, as usual!" said Keith.

"Shut the door!" said Barry crossly.

"No," said his brother, "I won't shut the door. I didn't leave it open. You shut it."

Neither brother would shut the shop door. They argued and argued and argued, hour after hour. . . . until it was quite dark and all the other shops had shut. All the shoppers had gone home but Barry and Keith kept on arguing.

When at last the town hall clock struck midnight, Keith said, "I know how to settle this argument. We will both sit here in silence until one of us speaks. The first one to speak must close the shop door. Do you agree?"

Barry agreed. So the two brothers sat in the dark in their shop, saying nothing.

At about one o'clock in the morning, two robbers came skulking down the high street. They couldn't believe their luck when they found the door of the jeweller's shop wide open. They slipped into the darkened shop and started to help themselves to all the gold and silver jewellery.

"Just look at all this lovely loot," said the first robber.

"Who says crime doesn't pay!" said the second.

The two brothers sat in the dark watching the robbers steal everything of value in the shop. But neither brother spoke. The robbers left, bent double under the weight of their haul, and still the brothers remained silent.

A few minutes later, two police officers came strolling down the high street. They saw the open door and came in to investigate. They could see that the shop had been robbed and when they saw Barry and Keith sitting in silence in the dark they thought they had caught the robbers red-handed.

"What's going on here?" said the first policeman.

The two brothers did not answer.

"What are you doing in this shop at two o'clock in the morning?" said the second policeman.

Still the two brothers would not speak.

The policemen got very angry and said that they would arrest Barry and Keith and lock them up for a very long time if they didn't answer their questions.

So Barry said, "We've been robbed."

As soon as he spoke, Keith jumped up and said, "I've won! I've won! You spoke first. You've got to shut the door!"

What to do

Read the six summaries. Only one fits the story. Which one is it? Say what is wrong with the other five summaries.

---

1   Two brothers argue over who should shut the shop door. Two policemen help them to settle the argument.

2   Two brothers were too busy arguing and did not see two robbers stealing everything in their shop.

3   The two brothers lost everything they owned because two foolish policemen could not catch some robbers.

4   The two brothers argued about closing the shop door. Barry was the first to speak so he closed it.

5   Everything was stolen from the stupid brothers' shop because they could not settle a foolish argument.

6   The two brothers argued so violently about closing the shop door that the police had to be called in.

The Fur Coat

Mrs Melrose was taking the night train from London to Glasgow. It was three o'clock in the morning and she was trying to sleep but couldn't. The heater wasn't working The compartment was very cold. Mrs Melrose had a very expensive fur coat. She wrapped it around her and curled up on the seat. There was only one other person in the compartment—a woman.

At about half past three in the morning Mrs Melrose left the compartment to get a drink. When she came back she got a nasty shock. The other woman was wearing her fur coat.

Mrs Melrose said, "How dare you! Give me back my coat at once, or I'll call the guard!"

The other woman just smiled and said it was her coat. So Mrs Melrose ran to get the guard.

The guard didn't know what to do. He had no idea who was the real owner of the fur coat. He said, "When we get into Glasgow I'd better take you both to the police."

An hour later Mrs Melrose and the other woman were in Glasgow Central Police Station. A young policewoman was trying to find out who owned the coat.

"It's mine!" said Mrs Melrose. "Look inside and you will see my name and address on the label."

When the policewoman looked inside the coat she couldn't find a label. The other woman had taken it out.

The policewoman said, "I must take this coat away and examine it."

She left the room and came back a few minutes later. She looked at both the women and said, "I am afraid the owner of

19

this coat is in very serious trouble. When I was examining the coat I found this inside the lining."

The policewoman held up a small plastic bag full of white powder. She said, "This is a very dangerous drug. The owner of this coat may go to prison for a long time."

When she heard this the other woman stood up and said, "Oh . . . well . . . perhaps I was wrong. It wasn't my coat after all." Then she left the police station as fast as she could.

Mrs Melrose was very upset. She said, "This is my coat. But I don't know anything about those drugs. That woman must have put them in the lining."

The policewoman handed Mrs Melrose her coat. She smiled and said, "Don't worry Mrs Melrose. I am sure you are the real owner of this coat. And by the way I didn't find anything in the lining. This is a packet of salt I borrowed from the canteen."

Are these sentences true, false or is there not enough evidence?

1 Mrs Melrose was travelling to Scotland.
2 She was going to Glasgow for a holiday.
3 She could not sleep because the compartment was crowded.
4 The other woman was from London.
5 Mrs Melrose left the compartment to go to the toilet.
6 The other woman took the coat at about half past three.
7 When Mrs Melrose called the guard the other woman panicked.
8 The guard took the two women to the police station in a taxi.
9 The thief had ripped the label out of the coat.
10 The two women had to wait hours while the coat was examined.
11 The policewoman pretended that one of the women was a drug dealer.
12 Mrs Melrose thought she was going to be arrested.

What to do next

Answer these questions. Give reasons.

1 Was the policewoman right to do what she did?
2 What might have gone wrong with her plan?
3 What other way might she have used to find the true owner of the fur coat?

Lost!

a story from Norway

"We're lost," said Ivar.

"No," said his brother Kris. "You're lost. I know where we are."

"Where are we then?" said Ivar. Kris did not answer.

"Where are we?" asked Ivar.

"Lost," said his brother, "but don't worry. The sun will be up in an hour or two. Let's just sit here and finish the bottle. A little drink will keep out the cold."

The two brothers were lost in a great forest. It was a starless night. There was no moon to guide them. They had been walking round and round in circles for three hours.

"What was that?" said Ivar suddenly.

"What was what?" said his brother.

"That noise. There, there it is again. There's something out there."

Then Kris heard it too: the sound of heavy footsteps coming towards them. A few seconds later they saw a huge dark shape moving through the trees nearby. When the shape spoke, it spoke not with one voice, but with three!

"I smell a human," said the first voice.

"I can't see him," said the second.

"Then give me the eye. Let me look," said the third.

As the dark shape came nearer, the brothers saw that it was three trolls—one-eyed giants who live in the mountains. They were holding on to each other, like drunks. As they came close to the brothers they understood why. The trolls had only got one eye between them!

"He's near. I can smell him," said the first troll.

"Here—you take the eye. See if you can spot him," said the second.

"Careful—don't drop it," said the third.

The brothers saw the second troll pluck the eye out of his head. He gave it to the first troll who put it into his empty eye socket.

"Come on," whispered Ivar. "Let's get out of here, before we end up in their cooking pot."

But Kris saw how to trick the trolls. He whispered, "We have nothing to fear from these three fools. We have four good eyes. They have only one. Let's play the fool with them. It will pass the time until sun-up."

Ivar was too frightened to argue. The trolls were very close now. He could hear their heavy breathing and smell their evil sweat.

"You run off to the left," whispered his brother, "and I'll go to the right. Make as much noise as you can. But do not speak."

Kris's trick worked. The first troll had the eye. He saw Ivar running to the left and said, "There he goes. Quickly this way! This way! But the second troll heard Kris running to the right and said, "No! No! There he goes. This way! This way!"

The brothers ran backwards and forwards between the trees. The trolls did not know which way to turn. They fell over, one after the other, with a crash. Then they began to argue over who should have the eye.

"Give it to me," shouted the second troll.

"No, it's my turn," said the third.

Round and round went the brothers. Backwards and forwards went the eye, until the brothers heard the first troll shout, "Oh no! I've dropped it."

Kris ran out from behind a tree and picked up the troll's eye. He laughed and said, "What did I tell you, Ivar? What fools these trolls are! Now we have five good eyes, and they have none."

"So—there are two of you," growled the first troll.

"Give us back our eye," snarled the second.

"Or we'll eat you—both," hissed the third.

"You'll have to catch us first," said Ivar. The trolls knew that they were powerless. The sun would be up soon. They had to get back to their cave in the mountains. A troll must never feel the sun's rays on his back, or he will be turned to stone.

"We'll give you gold," said the first troll suddenly.

"Yes, as much as you can carry," said the second.

"Look," said the third, and he shook his long black beard. Dozens of gold coins fell out onto the ground. The two brothers began to fill their pockets with gold, taking great care not to get too near the trolls. But as Ivar picked up the last coin, the first rays of the sun came dancing through the trees.

"Look!" said Kris.

The three trolls had turned into three great stones, leaning each against the others like three drunk men. The gold coins had turned to stone too. The two brothers emptied their pockets. They were full of pebbles: smooth, white round pebbles, each the size of a wide staring eye.

25

What to do

Read the five summaries. Only one fits the story. Which one is it? Say what is wrong with the other four summaries.

1   The story is about two boys who are turned to stone by three blind trolls.

2   The story is about two boys who are nearly caught and eaten by three blind giants.

3   The story is about two boys who are lost in a forest at night. They meet three trolls and steal some gold from them.

4   The story is about two boys who are nearly killed by three giants who have only one eye between them.

5   The story is about two boys who play a dangerous game with three one-eyed giants who turn to stone at dawn.

What to do next

Draw the scene in the forest "as the first rays of the sun came dancing through the trees".

CANNOCK CHASE
HIGH SCHOOL

Five More Minutes

It was Friday night and Andrew had been to the school disco. He got home at about eleven o'clock and watched the late night horror film, "Dracula's Revenge". It was well past midnight when he got to bed. He set the alarm clock because he had to get up at six the next morning.

Andrew's dad had a pie shop in town and Andrew helped him every Saturday. He had to be at the shop by seven at the latest. His dad went down to the shop at three o'clock in the morning to light up the ovens and make the pastry.

The alarm went off at ten to six. Andrew turned over and said to himself, "Five more minutes. . . . then I'll get up."

He woke up with a start at ten to seven. "Now I'm for it," he thought. His dad would be blazing mad. Saturday was a very busy day at the shop. People started to queue for pies before the shop opened at nine. The pies had to go into the oven by seven at the latest.

Andrew washed and dressed and ten minutes later was running down the road towards the shop. He got to the shop just as the town hall clock chimed half past seven.

He ran down the alley at the back of the shop. He tried to open the shop door but he couldn't. It wasn't locked. He could push it open a couple of centimetres, but no more. There was something heavy behind the door. His dad kept sacks of flour stacked up near the door. Andrew thought that a sack must have dropped down and blocked the door.

He banged on the door and shouted, "Dad! Dad! It's me, Andy. I'm sorry I'm late. I can't get in. There's a sack up against the door."

There was no answer. Andrew pushed the door open a few centimetres and put his mouth to the gap.

"Dad! Are you there?" he shouted.

It was then that Andrew smelled the gas. He knew right away what had happened. It wasn't a sack of flour behind the door. It was his dad! Something must have gone wrong with the pie oven. The shop was full of gas. His dad must have passed out trying to get out into the fresh air.

Andrew pushed the door with all his might. It opened a bit more but sprung back again. His father was a big man and he was lying hard up against the door. Andrew couldn't move him. He'd have to get help.

He ran down the passage and out into the street. But the street was deserted. He ran back to the shop door and tried again. This time it opened a little bit wider. He could see into the back of the shop. He could see his dad's boots, white with flour and his long white apron. He pushed with all his might and now the gap was wide enough for him to squeeze into the shop.

He rolled his dad away from the door, but within seconds he felt sick and dizzy himself. The room began to spin. Suddenly there were three doors and they were spinning like a fairground ride. He heard a voice in his head saying, "I must get off. I must stop the ride. I've got to open the door!" But which door? Now there were a dozen doors, all spinning like tops. He closed his eyes and reached out like a blind person. He pulled the door open and rolled his father out into the passage. He tried to give him the kiss of life, but fell back sick and crying. The ride began to spin again and this time he could not make it stop.

When Andrew came round, he was in the back of an ambulance. He was lying under a red blanket. His father was in the ambulance too. An ambulance man was holding an oxygen mask to his father's face. Andrew tried to sit up, but couldn't.

"Lie still, son," said the ambulance man. "Your dad will be all right. Just lie still now."

"But how did you know?" said Andrew. "We were both unconscious."

"The postman found you," said the ambulance man. "He smelled gas at the front of the shop and went round the back to investigate. Did you pull your dad out?"

Andrew nodded.

"He had a very lucky escape, your dad," said the ambulance man. "Five more minutes in that shop. . . ."

Andrew lay back and closed his eyes. He was suddenly very cold. He started to shiver and sweat. He was thinking of those five more minutes he'd had in bed that morning. Thanks to Count Dracula he'd been on the right side of the shop door.

What to do

You are a newspaper reporter and you have been sent to interview Andrew and his father about the accident. Write a report to go with the following headline:

Dracula saves father and son

You should draw a diagram so that readers can see clearly what happened at the shop. Label it.

The Ghost that Could Not Rest

a story from China

Yun Lo was a lazy old man who never did any work and drank too much. Late one night he was going home from the inn. He saw a strange woman in the lane ahead of him. She was dressed all in white and carrying a long thick rope. She moved very quickly and very quietly like a cat.

Who was she? Where was she going? Yun watched her go into the house of Mrs Lee. Mrs Lee lived by herself. Two years ago her husband had gone away and never returned. Mrs Lee was very unhappy. No one could cheer her up. She never came out of her house. She had locked herself away from the world.

"What does this strange woman in white want with Mrs Lee?" Yun said to himself. He crept up to her house and looked in at the window. He could see Mrs Lee and the woman standing in the middle of the living room. There was a long thick rope hanging down from a beam. In the end of the rope was a noose!

"What on earth's going on?" muttered Yun.

Mrs Lee seemed to be in a dream, as if she was sleepwalking. She was moving towards the noose. . . . and putting her head into it! Then Yun understood what was happening.

"Help! Help!" he shouted at the top of his voice. "Someone's trying to murder Mrs Lee!"

Yun made such a row that he woke up the whole village. The people came running out of their houses. The woman in white slipped away into the shadows. So the villagers took hold of Yun and said, "Drunk again, Yun!" Then they beat him with sticks and chased him off home.

Yun was sure he had seen a woman in white. He was also sure that Mrs Lee had been in great danger. But who would listen to an old drunk?

When Yun was near his home he saw the strange woman in white again. She was in the lane, just ahead of him and she was carrying the same long thick rope. Yun ran up behind her and grabbed her by the arm.

"Who are you?" said Yun. But she would not answer. He twisted her arm and said, "Why did you try to make Mrs Lee kill herself?" But still the woman would not answer.

"Answer me," said Yun, getting cross, "or I'll take you to the police."

The woman in white laughed and said, "You old fool! There isn't a cell on earth that can hold me. I'm not like you, old man. I am from that awful place half way between this world and the world of spirits. I died a violent death—murdered by my own daughter. Because of this I can never rest. I must wander the Earth forever. . . . unless. . . ."

"Unless what?" said Yun.

"Unless I can get someone to take my place," she cried as she slipped her long thick rope round Yun's kneck. She pulled on the rope with the strength of ten women. She laughed and said, "Now old fool you will take my place in the world of the Undead."

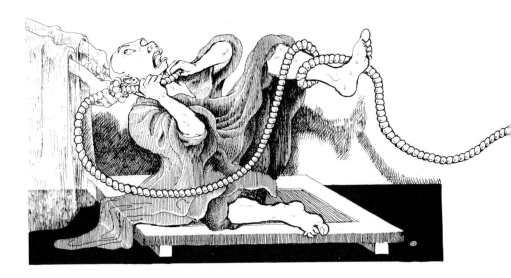

Yun fought like a tiger. He pulled the rope from his neck and called out, "Help! Police! Murder!"

Once again he woke up the whole village. And once again the woman in white slipped away into the night. When the villagers found Yun, all alone, sitting in the road outside his house they said, "Drunk again! Lock him up!"

The next morning at dawn the policeman brought Yun some tea. He said, "Here you are, old man, breakfast."

Yun drank the tea slowly and watched the sun rise over the village.

"What happened last night?" Yun asked the policeman. "It's like a bad dream." The policeman just smiled and shook his head.

By noon Yun was free to go. On his way home he went past the inn. It was full of noisy drinkers who called out to him, "Yun Lo, come and join us!"

But Yun walked quickly on down the road, and never once looked back.

┌─ **What to do** ──────────────────────────────────

Copy the sketch map of the village.
Label it to show where the main events of the story took place
and who was involved.

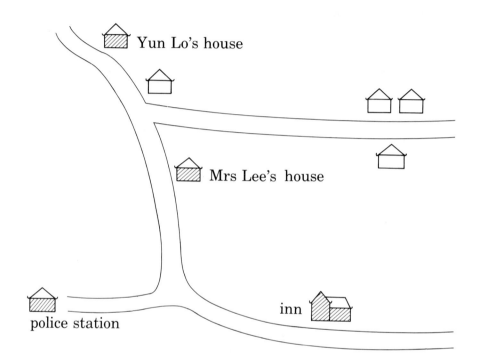

Yun Lo's house

Mrs Lee's house

police station

inn

┌─ **What to do next** ──────────────────────────────

Make a list of all the clues in the story that tell you about the
woman in white.
Write your answers like this:

1. She was dressed all in white.

2.

The Lost Ruby

a story from India

There was once a king who was always sad. He never laughed or smiled. Nothing seemed to please him. He always looked on the dark side of life.

The king had a large house with a wonderful garden. An old man looked after the garden. He had worked in the garden since he was a small boy. He was always singing as he worked.

One day the king was walking in his garden when he heard the old man's song amongst the roses. He called him over.

"Tell me, old man," said the king, "why are you always so cheerful?"

The old man said, "Sadness can never enter my heart. I have locked it out."

"Don't be stupid!" said the king crossly. "Your heart is not a house! No one can escape sadness."

The old man just smiled and went back to his roses.

The king was angry with the old man. He decided to prove that he was right, and the old gardener was wrong.

The next day the king went down into the garden again. He took a large ruby from his pocket and gave it to the old gardener. "I want you to look after this for me," he said. "But I must warn you, old man, that if you lose this ruby you will lose your life as well."

The old man took the ruby home and hid it under his bed. That night the king, disguised as a beggar, went to the gardener's house and stole the ruby. He took it and threw it into the river.

The next day the king went down into his garden again. He

called the old man over and said, "I want you to bring that ruby to the palace in two days time. And remember, if you lose it . . ."

When the old man got home that night, the first thing he did was look under his bed. When he saw that the ruby had been stolen he knew he had only two days to live.

"Two short days," he said with a sigh. "I'd better make the most of them."

He decided to sell his house and use the money to give a party for all his friends. He told them he was going away—but did not tell them where or when.

When the king heard about the party, he once again disguised himself as a beggar and went to the old man's house. When he arrived, he had to go to the back gate because there was such a crush of friends and neighbours at the front. There were well-wishers everywhere: on the stairs, in the kitchen, round the well. The house was buzzing like one of the hives in the king's garden.

The king slipped into the living room and found a space on the floor in the corner. He sat down to listen and watch. One by one the guests wished the old man well and drank his health. The king never took his eyes off the gardener. But there was never a shadow of sadness in the old man's face or a whisper of pain in his voice.

When all the toasts had been drunk the old man carried in a great wooden platter. On it were twelve silver fish on a bed of flowers.

"Come," said the old man, "eat, eat!"

"It's a feast fit for a king," said his neighbour.

The old man sliced up the fish one by one and gave each guest a helping. When he sliced open the twelfth fish he found a large ruby. The guests were amazed when he held it up.

"It's a king's ransom," said his neighbour.

"Oh yes," said the gardener, "a ransom right enough."

The next day the old man went to the palace and asked to see the king. The king knew he had been wrong to try to trick the old man, so he told him the truth.

"You are right, old man," he said. "Your heart is a house and you have locked sadness out. It is you who has taught me the lesson. Take the ruby—keep it. A small reward."

The gardener thanked the king and slipped the ruby into his apron pocket, along with the seeds and string and pruning knife. He sold the ruby and bought a new house—a bigger house with a large garden. Over the door he hung a sign:

This door is open to all—but sadness.

What to do

Are these sentences probably true (PT), definitely true (DT), probably false (PF), definitely false (DF) or is there no evidence (NE)?

1 The king was never happy, even when he was a child.

2 The gardener knew a great deal about plants.

3 The king's favourite flowers were red roses.

4 Nothing sad had ever happened to the gardener.

5 The king thought the gardener was a stupid old fool.

6 The gardener knew the real reason why the king had given him the ruby.

7 The king paid a beggar to steal the ruby from the gardener.

8 When the gardener knew he had only had two days to live he was very scared.

9 Most of the people in the village went to the gardener's farewell party.

10 The king thought the gardener would break down and cry at the party.

11 The king told the old man who had stolen the ruby.

12 In the end the gardener felt very bitter towards the king.

What to do next

The king says, "It is you who has taught me a lesson. . . ." What lesson do you think the old gardener had taught the king?

The Storm

It was Christmas Eve and we were on our way down to Stoke-on-Trent by car. My sister's husband, Jeff, was driving and I was in the back with my sister Marie. Marie's baby, Sophie, was fast asleep in her carry cot next to us.

As we hurried down the motorway, Jeff had the car radio on. He was worried because the weather forecast said there was going to be a heavy snow fall. It was a windy night too, so the snow would pile up in drifts and make things even worse.

Jeff drove as fast as he could because he wanted to get to Stoke before it snowed. We got to the turn off for Stoke just after 7.30. We turned off the motorway and saw a sign:

Stoke-on-Trent   7 miles

"Not long now," said Jeff.

"I'd hate to get stuck on the motorway in a blizzard," said Marie, "especially with a baby in the car."

We were about five miles from Stoke when it started to rain. It was a very cold night and the east wind blew in great gusts across the road, making driving very difficult. Soon the rain turned to snow and the windscreen was plastered with huge snowflakes. Jeff was driving very slowly as he could only just see the tail lights of the car in front. I was worried and so was Marie.

She said, "Drive carefully Jeff."

"It's okay," he said. "Not far now."

"How can you see where to go?" I asked. "I can't see anything through the windscreen."

"I'm following the tail lights of the car in front," said Jeff. "I hope he knows where he's going!"

Then, without warning, the car in front skidded in the snow. The driver braked hard and the red glow of his brake lights lit up our windscreen. Jeff tried to stop, but it was no use. There was a sickening crash as we hit the car in front.

I was thrown on to the floor and Sophie's carry cot slipped down on top of me. She started to cry so I picked her up.

"Give her to me," said Marie. "She's a bit upset, that's all. Are you all right?"

"Yes," I said, "but what about the people in the other car. It's gone into the ditch I think."

"I'll take a look," said Jeff. "You stay here out of the cold."

Jeff struggled through the deep snow to the other car. It was half off the road with its front wheels in a deep ditch. The driver was unconscious. The windscreen was shattered and the dashboard was covered in blood.

Jeff came back to our car and got his overcoat out of the boot.

"I've got to get help," he said. "There must be a house nearby. You sit tight. I'll not be long."

By now the road was half a metre deep in snow so no cars could get along it. Jeff knew he had to get to a 'phone quickly or the injured man might die.

After Jeff had been gone about five minutes, Marie gave me the baby and said, "Hold Sophie while I see what I can do for that chap in the car. Don't let her get cold now." Then she pulled on her thick leather coat and went out into the snow.

I was left alone with Sophie. It was getting cold in the car because the wind seemed to find its way through every little crack. The heater was on but it wasn't working very well because the car wasn't moving.

After a few minutes Sophie woke up and started to cry. She was getting cold. I looked out of the window to see if Marie was coming back but all I could see was a blurr of white flakes.

41

I rocked the baby, talked to her, sang her a lullaby, but she wouldn't stop crying. Her hands and face felt quite cold. I tried to wind down the window to shout to Marie but it was frozen tight. I tried to open the door but that was held fast by snow blown up against the side of the car.

Then I remembered a story I'd read at school about a Russian woman who had kept her baby alive in an awful Siberian blizzard. She'd put her baby inside her clothes next to her skin.

I took off my coat and undid my cardigan, pulled up my vest and put Sophie against my skin. Even though my hands and face were cold, my chest was very warm. I tucked her hands under my armpits and her feet down the front of my knickers. Then I covered her over with my cardigan and coat and she stopped crying.

Just then I heard Marie banging on the car roof and shouting, "Jenny! Are you all right? I can't get the door open."

"I'm okay," I called. "What's happening?"

"Don't worry Jenny," she said. "Jeff's back. He'll get you out of there."

The next thing I knew, I was being picked up with Sophie still warm against me and wrapped in a blanket. There were people all around. Strange voices, strange faces, torches and flashing lights.

Then I was lifted up into the cab of a lorry and Marie climbed in beside me. She slipped her hand inside my blanket, smiled and said, "Sophie's warm as toast."

"Will she be all right?" I said.

"Oh yes," said my sister. "You've kept her warm enough. But what about you? Are you all right Jenny?"

"I am now," I said and I pressed my face hard against the blanket so my sister wouldn't see that I was crying.

The lorry was a gritting truck with a huge snow plough on the front and it took us to the police station at Stoke-on-Trent where Jeff had to make a statement about the accident.

The driver of the other car survived the crash. His life had been saved by my sister Marie although I didn't know this until the sergeant at the police station told me.

"She's a very brave person, your sister," he said. "She saved his life you know because she gave him her coat, then sat out there in the bitter cold with him till that plough got through."

Marie just smiled and said, "Anyone would have done the same. I wouldn't call it brave." Then she came over to me and put her arm around me.

"Here's the real hero of the night, my young sister. Jenny had the hardest job—keeping Sophie happy. How is she Jenny?"

I slipped my hand under the blanket and felt the baby warm against my chest. "Still fast asleep," I said.

"Do you want me to take her for a bit?" said my sister. "You look very tired."

"No," I said. "I'm all right, honest."

My back was stiff and my arms were aching but I could have held my little niece for ever.

Draw a diagram to show the scene of the accident when Jeff returned with help. Label it clearly to show Jenny, the baby, Marie, the injured man, Jeff and the snow plough, and any other important details.

Answer these questions.

1 Say how the lives of two people were saved and by whom.
2 Who do *you* think was to blame for the accident? Give reasons.

A Bed for the Night

a story from Ireland

Pat Diver lived in Ireland. He was a tinker who went from town to town mending pots and pans and kettles. One day Pat was in a lonely part of Donegal, a long way from home. It was getting dark and he was looking for somewhere to sleep. There were a few small cottages along the road. Pat went to one and said, "Can I have a bed for the night?"

The owner of the cottage said, "Have you a story to tell? We will give you a bed for the night only if you can tell us a story."

But Pat Diver had no story to tell.

Pat went to every cottage along the lonely road. At each cottage he was asked the same question: "Have you a story to tell?" At each cottage Pat had to give the same sorry answer.

So that night Pat had to sleep in an old barn. He curled up under some straw and went to sleep. He woke up some time later when he heard heavy footsteps near the barn. He peeped out from under the straw and saw four very tall men coming into the barn. They were carrying a dead body. Pat lay still under the straw. He hardly dared breathe.

The four tall men lit a fire in the middle of the barn. Then they hung the body over the fire from a beam in the roof. They were going to roast it!

The four men started to argue. Who was going to watch the body while it cooked? They argued and argued. Their voices were so loud and angry that slates fell off the barn roof.

Then all of a sudden one of the tall men said, "We are silly to stand here arguing. There's Pat Diver hiding under the straw— why don't we get him to watch the roast!"

Pat jumped up and tried to run away. But there was no

escape from the four tall men. They made Pat sit by the fire and turn the roast. Then they went off to search for some potatoes and greens.

Pat was so frightened that he did not know what to do. He could not bear to touch the dead body. Soon the rope caught fire and burned through. The body fell with a mighty crash into the fire. Pat ran for his life.

He ran over fields and through hedges. He ran through rivers and woods. When he could run no further he lay down in a muddy ditch by a lonely track. "I've escaped," he said to himself. But he was wrong . . . for at that very moment the four tall men came down the lonely track. They were carrying the half-cooked body. They were arguing over who should carry it. They stopped right next to the spot where Pat Diver was hiding. One of the men said, "We are silly to stand here arguing. There's Pat Diver hiding in the ditch—why don't we get him to carry our roast!"

This time Pat did not try to run away. He climbed out of the ditch and took the body on his shoulder without a word. The four tall men took Pat and the half-cooked body to an old graveyard. They began to dig a grave.

"Quick," said one of the men, looking up at the sky. "The sun will be up soon."

They dug and dug for half an hour. The grave was very deep and very wide.

"That grave is big enough for two bodies," thought Pat. So when the four men weren't looking, he ran for his life. He ran and ran and ran. He didn't stop running until he saw the first rays of the sun in the east. Then he knew he was safe from the four tall men.

The next day Pat Diver was back in his home town. It was the time of the summer fair and the town was crowded with strangers. Pat was standing in the town square. He was watching the farmers buying and selling horses.

All of a sudden Pat saw one of the four tall men coming towards him through the crowd.

"Why, hello Pat," said the tall man, "and how are you today?" Pat was too scared to answer.

"Are you thinking of buying a horse Pat?" asked the tall man. Still Pat was too frightened to answer.

"Have you forgotten how to speak Pat?" asked the tall man with a wink. Pat didn't answer.

"Ah well," said the tall man, "I'd better be on my way. Who knows, Pat Diver, we might meet again. And remember the next time you want a bed for the night in lonely Donegal you'll have a fine story to tell, won't you!"

The tall man slipped away into the crowd. Pat the Tinker never saw him or his three friends again. But he was never, ever refused a bed for the night in lonely Donegal.

What to do

Draw a diagram to show the journey Pat made and all the things that happened to him. This key will help you. Use these symbols in your diagram.

cottage		wood	
barn		fields/hedges	
river		graveyard	
track		town	
ditch			

The Dark Divide

When I got home from school I found the back door wide open. The kitchen was in darkness. The radio was on. The fire was out. I switched on the light and saw the table cluttered with unwashed breakfast things.

"Mum? Mum? Where are you?"

No answer.

I went through into the living room. My father was home. That was unusual. He was never home much before six. He was sitting alone in the dark by the fire.

"Where's Mum?" I said. He didn't answer.

I stood there, holding my school bag, waiting, expecting the worst.

"She's gone," he said at last, "to live with Paul. She's gone for good this time. She's never coming back." I sat down beside him on the sofa. He put his arm round me. We sat there in silence for a long time.

"I'd better make the tea," my father said at last getting up and switching on the light.

"Where's Shaun?" I said. "Does he know?"

"Yes," said my father. "He's in his room. Go up and see if he's all right will you? I thought I heard him crying before."

Shaun was crying. He cried for hours. I was scared. I thought he might die. I know that's a stupid idea. But he seemed to be getting thinner, crying himself hollow. Nothing I could do or say would stop the tears. I was his big tough sister—he called me his Minder. But I couldn't stop the tears. I sat on his bed and put my arms round him. He fell asleep in my arms. But he was a million miles away. He was on the other side of a dark divide. And I could not reach him.

*   *   *

When Dad asked Shaun what he wanted to do—where he wanted to live—he couldn't answer. He stood there like a puppet waiting for a jerk of the strings.

I said, "Do you want to go and live with Mum and Paul?"

Shaun nodded, a slow wooden nod.

I stayed with my father. Not because I loved him more than my mother. I stayed with him out of fear. Fear of leaving the security of our old house. Fear of crossing that dark divide between the familiar and the unknown.

My father said, "But you've never met Paul, have you? Don't you want to meet him, then make up your mind? Your mother would like that."

"What would you do," I said, "if you were me?"

He didn't answer.

"All right," I said, "I'll go—this Sunday."

*   *   *

My mum opened the door. "Come in. Come in," she said taking my duffle coat. Was it that that made me cry? Hearing her say, "Come in?" Hearing her say something so ordinary. Hearing her talk to me like a . . . stranger. She seemed far away. She was a shadow in the shadows. She was a mile away across that dark divide.

"Don't cry," she said. "You'll upset your brother." She dried my eyes, then pushed me into the living room. Shaun was sitting on the rug by the fire playing with his Action Man. Paul was sitting in an arm chair with his back to the door. My mum said, "Paul, this is Christine, my daughter." Paul stood up. A cigarette lighter fell out of his lap and clattered into the grate. It wasn't until he bent down and tried to pick it up that I realised he was blind. Shaun found the lighter, picked it up and pressed it into Paul's hand.

51

Paul turned towards Mum and me and said, "I'm pleased to meet you, Christine." He held out his hand for me to shake. I shook his hand and he said, "I didn't realise you were so tall. I'd pictured you as much smaller."

"I'm nearly twelve," I said, suddenly feeling like a freak.

"She's nearly as tall as our dad," said Shaun.

Paul smiled. He let go of my hand. He sat down and lit a cigarette.

Mum went out to make some tea. Paul did most of the talking. He asked me about school, about the netball team, the computer club, my new bike, the cat. He seemed to know all about me. He had bright blue eyes. They seemed to look right inside me. He seemed to know what I was going to say before I said it—so I didn't say much.

When it was time to leave, Paul stood up and put out his hand. I held out my hand too—thinking he wanted to shake hands again. But instead he put his hand to my face.

"May I?" he said. "Then I'll have a picture in my head." I looked to my mother. She was willing me to say "Yes".

"All right," I said in barely a whisper.

Paul ran his hand gently over my face. I could smell the cigarette smoke on his fingers. When he touched my eyes he said, "You've been crying," and he took his hand away.

"Come on," said my mother, "it's time you were going. Your dad will have your tea ready. Will we see you next weekend?"

"Yes," I said pulling on my duffle coat and slipping out into the hall. Shaun opened the front door for me. It was quite dark outside now.

"Aren't you scared of the dark?" Shaun asked. "Aren't you scared going home alone in the dark."

"No—there are street lights all the way," I said, trying to sound grown-up.

"But the dark bits in between," said Shaun, "what about them? I'm scared of them."

"No, of course not," I said. Then I kissed my mother goodbye and left without another word.

What to do

Copy the table and fill it in.
How did they feel?

		happy	sad	scared	nervous	angry
1	Christine, when she came home from school.	1				
2	Shaun, when he went up to his room.	2				
3	Christine, when she went to see Shaun in his room.	3				
4	Shaun, when he had to choose where to live.	4				
5	The father, when Christine decided to stay with him.	5				
6	Christine, when she met Paul.	6				
7	Paul, when Christine came into the room.	7				
8	Christine, when Paul touched her face.	8				
9	The mother, when Christine was leaving.	9				
10	Christine, as she walked home alone.	10				

What to do

Paul had never met Christine before. How did he try to make a picture of her in his head? What sorts of clues can blind persons use to build up mental pictures of people they meet?

A Hundred Thousand Keys

a story from India

The old man was dying. His three sons stood by his bed. No one spoke. The only sound was the rasp of the old man's breathing, like a cold wind turning dead leaves.

Just after midnight the old man sat up and called out, "A light! Bring me a light!"

The oldest son said, "There's a candle at the bedside, father. And one at the window and another by the door."

The old man put out his hands like a blind person, and said, "Who's there? Why are we sitting in the dark?"

"We are all here with you, father," said the second son.

"And we've each lit a candle for you," said the third.

An hour later the old man asked for pen and paper. When a pen was pressed into his hand he said, "I can see only ink, a sea of ink. Which way is the shore? I'm drowning. Help me!"

The youngest son took the old man's hand and said, "Let me help, father. Tell me what to write."

The will was a simple one. The old man had nothing of value except his camels. The will said how they should be divided.

"My oldest son shall have half the camels. My second son shall have one third of the camels. My youngest son shall have one ninth of the camels."

The old man signed the will, and died.

After the funeral the three sons met to divide up the camels. They were all fine strong beasts with thick brown fur. The youngest son led them into the yard behind their father's house. There were seventeen of them.

When they tried to divide the camels they found it was impossible. They could all read and write but they knew little about numbers. They tried counting on their fingers, sharing out stones and nuts, making marks in the dust—but no matter how they tried, it could not be done.

The oldest son began to lose his temper. He said, "What a stupid old man he was! If I am to have half his camels I must chop one of them in two!"

The other two sons would not agree to this. They began to argue. They started to shout and swear and fight. They rolled about in the dust between the camels' legs like a pack of dogs. They called each other, "Trickster, Fool, Liar, Cheat."

Just as the youngest son was about to pull out his knife, the gate swung open and a stranger walked into the yard. When he saw the three sons rolling in the dust he said, "My young friends, your poor father will rise from his grave. I could hear your anger a thousand miles away. Let your father rest in peace!"

"Who are you?" said the youngest son.

"I was a good friend of your father a long time ago. I have come to say some words over his grave. Will you show me the way?"

The three brothers took the stranger to the grave. They watched him place some flowers there and heard him say these words: "There are a thousand roads to heaven. At the end of each road are ten thousand doors. Every door has a hundred keys. I wish you a safe journey my old friend."

The stranger stood looking down at the grave for a long time.

Back at the house the stranger asked the brothers why they had been quarrelling. They told him about the will, and the seventeen camels that would not be divided.

The stranger smiled and went out into the lane by the house. He came back leading an old white camel. He brought it into the yard and tied it up with the other camels.

"A gift," he said, "in memory of your father, my friend."

Without saying another word the stranger left the yard, closing the gate quietly behind him.

The three brothers were even more confused. They hadn't been able to agree on how to share out their father's camels and now there was the white camel. How was that to be shared?

It was the youngest son who found the answer first, as if a candle had been lit in the dark cave of his brain.

"Now I understand!" he cried. "Now we have eighteen camels!"

"True," said the eldest son. "So if I take half the camels I will have nine."

"And if I take one third," said the second son, "I can have six."

"And my share is one ninth," said the youngest, "so I will take two."

When they had shared out the camels there was one camel left, the old white camel—the gift from the stranger.

"Who is to have this camel?" said the eldest son. "Is it mine?"

"No," said the youngest.

"Then is it mine?" asked the second.

"No," said the youngest. "Don't you see, it belongs to all of us, to everyone, to the whole world!"

The other brothers still did not understand.

"It belongs to nobody," said the youngest brother, "like the sky or the rain or the light from the moon. It belongs to nobody. . . . so it belongs to us all."

What to do

Draw a diagram to show how the three sons solved their problem. Label it clearly showing how the camels were finally divided.

What to do next

Make a list of all the things that *you* think "belong to nobody . . . so belong to us all." Start with the three things in the story and add as many others as you can.

The Man Leopard

a story from Nigeria

There was once a young man called Uzo who wanted to be a great hunter. He went to a witch-doctor and said, "Make me the best hunter in the village."

The witch-doctor gave Uzo a powerful drink made from herbs and said, "This will make you the best hunter in the world."

Uzo drank the bitter drink. Then the witch-doctor said, "Be warned Uzo. From now on you must hunt only at night. And you must always hunt alone."

The next night Uzo went out to hunt. He went alone as he had been told. As soon as he was a little way from the village, he changed into a leopard! At first he was very frightened. He did not understand what was happening to him. He wanted to run away and hide. Then he remembered what the witch-doctor had said, " . . . the best hunter in the world. . . . "

The bitter drink had made Uzo so fast and so strong that he could catch and kill any animal, just like the leopard.

That night Uzo caught and killed a great wild pig and took it back to his village. The next night and every night he slipped out alone to hunt. Every morning there was always meat outside his hut.

Uzo soon became famed as a hunter. All the other hunters wanted to know his secret but he would not tell them. The drums spoke his name in every village. He had no equal as a hunter. Children stood on his shadow for luck. He could sit and drink with the old men. There were a thousand stories about his skill as a hunter. The young men called him "Spear that sees in the dark".

A year passed and it was time for Uzo to marry. He could

have married any one of a hundred girls but he loved Akim. She lived in the next village. Uzo had known her since they were children.

One day Uzo decided to go and ask Akim if she would marry him. When he got near to her village he saw Akim swimming in the river. He ran down to the river, shouting, "Akim! Akim! It's me, Uzo!"

But as he ran through the long grass by the river he could feel himself changing into the leopard. There was nothing he could do. A dark force turned his blood to fire and he sprang on Akim and pulled her out of the river.

She ran off screaming, "Help me! Help me! A leopard!"

She was bleeding. Uzo had cut her back with his sharp claws. She fled in fear to her own village and Uzo fled in shame to hide in the forest.

The next day Uzo went back to the witch-doctor. He told him what had happened by the river. Uzo said, "How can I stop myself from hurting those I love?"

The witch-doctor stared into the fire for a long time and then said, "I can stop you from hurting those you love. It can be done, but there is a price."

"I'll give you anything," said Uzo. "What do you want? My hut? My spears? My gold neck band?"

The witch-doctor shook his head and said, "I want the thing you value more than anything else."

Uzo frowned and said, "I don't understand. . . . "

"You will, Uzo," said the witch-doctor, "tomorrow."

Then he handed Uzo a small dark bottle. "Drink this tonight," he said. "This will kill the leopard in your heart."

That night Uzo lay down on the grass outside his hut. He looked up at the stars and thought, "Will I ever see these stars again, or the moon over the river, or Akim?"

He remembered then that terrible moment by the river when his claws bit into Akim's back. He knew what he must do. He must kill the leopard once and for all. So he took out the small dark bottle and drank the bitter drink.

When Uzo closed his eyes on the moon and stars he did not expect to see them again. But the next morning he was woken from a deep sleep by a dog licking his nose. Then he heard his neigbour laugh and say, "Look at Uzo! He has the best hut in the village and he sleeps in the grass!"

The witch-doctor had spoken the truth. Uzo never again changed into a leopard. Very soon he knew the price he had had to pay. It was his name. When he went out to hunt, all he could catch were rabbits. "Uzo the Great," "Uzo the fearless," "Uzo the spear that sees in the dark" soon became just ordinary Uzo. That was the price the witch-doctor had spoken of.

But as the years passed Uzo won another name. He became known as Uzo the Wise. He was a bad hunter but a good friend. Young and old came to him with their problems. He saw some good in everyone and so everyone saw good in him.

Some years later Uzo married Akim. They had seven strong children. At night Akim, Uzo and their children would sit by the fire under the stars and Uzo would tell them stories. He was a wonderful storyteller. When he had finished his stories the children always wanted to hear Akim's story.

"Tell us about your scars," they would say. "Tell us about the terrible leopard. . . . "

Akim's story always made Uzo cry. But he hid his tears from his wife and children. Uzo was a man and men do not cry.

What to do

Read the six summaries. Only one fits the story. Which one is it? Say what is wrong with the other five summaries.

---

1   A witch-doctor helps a poor young man called Uzo to kill a leopard.

2   A young man is helped by a clever witch-doctor to discover something very important about himself.

3   A young man called Uzo thinks he is mad because he believes he has a leopard inside him.

4   A young man called Uzo gives up the chance to be rich, famous and powerful so that he can marry a girl called Akim.

5   A famous hunter called Uzo is changed into a leopard by a witch-doctor and killed by hunters.

6   A young man called Uzo kills a leopard that lives in his heart, then marries a girl called Akim.

Note to the teacher

Headwork Stories can be used in two ways:

a) They can be used as a collection of short, readable stories to be read purely for pleasure. To this end they can be taped by the teacher for individual listening.

b) They can be seen also as a resource to supplement the parallel series *Headwork 1–4*, and *English Headwork 1–4* because they set out (through the exercises linked to the stories) to reinforce the same skills as the *Headwork* books. They also attempt, like *Headwork*, to help the pupils find a challenge in the necessary routine of practising basic reading skills. With this in mind the stories, though written in a readable style, are not all simple. Most make quite subtle demands on the reader's reasoning. (There are, after all, many poor readers who respond very intelligently to a complex story read to them.) Many of the stories, therefore, require the reader to speculate about issues such as revenge, bravery, life after death, aggression, loyalty, competition and co-operation.

Most of the stories are short but there are a number of quite long stories in each collection and reading these should help pupils develop the confidence to tackle longer prose works.

As with *Headwork 1–4* the written outcomes have been kept to a minimum in favour of tasks which challenge the pupils' intelligence and thereby encourage them to *read and re-read* the text reflectively.

Skill emphasised	Story
Deduction	1 3 ⑤ 9 10
Summaries	4 6 14
Writing	① 3 **7**
Drawing	2 6 8 10 11 ⑬
Assessing evidence	8
Motive/feeling	**12**

Story numbers printed in **bold** indicate tasks which require teacher explanation. Numbers circled indicate tasks with open-ended outcomes.